THE BOOK "PROMOTE & PROSPER: STRATEGIES TO BUSINESS GROWTH"

Contents

3

FORWARD

What is marketing for businesses?

To reach their target audiences, convey messages to them, and increase the sale of products and services, many organizations and companies utilize a variety of marketing tactics, such as company promotion. To accomplish their goal, they could use a variety of strategies, including PR, personal selling, and direct marketing. By choosing the best marketing strategy for your company, you may boost profits and establish a solid reputation. The definition of business promotion, the distinctions between it and advertising, and a discussion of its many forms are all covered in this article.

What is marketing for businesses?

You may research what it comprises and its many varieties to get the answer to the question "What is business promotion?" Businesses utilize business promotion as a method to boost sales of their goods and services. It's a part of the marketing mix, which also includes the elements of product, price, venue, and promotion. Utilizing a variety of platforms is part of business marketing, which aims to inspire customers to make purchases.

Advertising and company promotion have different purposes.

The precise categories that company marketing and advertising fall under are only one of the variations between them. Additional distinctions include:

Definition

The goal of business marketing is to enhance sales by influencing people to purchase things. Flyers, social media, and direct person-to-person selling are some of the ways businesses do this. Advertising provides information to people about a product or service through a sponsored network, such television commercials. A part of company marketing is advertising.

Aims

The goal of the company promotion is to encourage customers who are already familiar with a product, service, or brand to make purchases. This exercise's primary goal is to increase sales. Consumers who may or may not be aware of a certain brand are reached via advertising. Building a brand's reputation is advertising's primary goal. Strategies for business promotion have effect right away, while advertising's effects may not be felt for some time.

Technique

While company promotion is more direct, advertising takes an indirect technique to spreading awareness of a product.

What Is The Target Market?

A target audience is a certain demographic that is most likely to purchase your product or service. As seen in the graphic below, it lies at the center of all your targeting and advertising plans.

It varies from persona targeting—ideal groupings of individuals who make ideal customers—which is significantly wider and covers groups that "may be interested."

Typical Target Audiences

A smart strategy to make sure you're connecting with and impacting individuals who will most likely become clients is by defining your target demographic.

BMW, for instance, has a certain target market for which it provides a variety of automobiles (and now experiences) built around "The Ultimate Driving Machine."

Although BMW has a reputation for having very loyal consumers, it also actively seeks out new ones. Although wealthy clients are the company's main target market, it also advertises to a wide variety of people worldwide.

How to Find and Connect with Your Target Audience

Every business needs to have an idea of who their target market is, but in B2B marketing, it can be especially helpful to develop target personas that go much further. Here, you can use research-based profiles that identify your potential customers to help create content specifically for them and their needs.

Effective Ways to Assist In Creating a Great Brand Identity?

Modern customers want connections with a company's brand's voice, message, and appearance rather than simply a specific product. However, creating a brand is a process rather than a single action. Owners of companies need to choose the best strategies for marketing their brand identity as well as too continually "live" it in addition to knowing their job and consumers.

Focus Your Brand on Your Narrative

Smart consumers search for opportunities to relate to and identify with the goods and services they purchase. Finding oneself in your origin story is a powerful approach for consumers to develop that connection with your brand. Your company's genesis narrative should explain the inspiration for its development in a manner that your target clients can identify with it and develop a sense of loyalty toward you.

Make sure the customer is satisfied Complies with Brand Promise

Take into account how the actual consumer experience reflects the brand promise. How, for instance, are the customer's touch points reflecting the brand promise's focus on trust? Does simply the penalty for not paying appear on your invoice? How does that fulfill the commitment? It's critical to think about how each stage of the client journey is connected to your brand.

Make certain your team members adore you.

Leaders of organizations often overlook the reality that their staff members are their largest brand ambassadors. They will enhance their brand more than they anticipated if they treat their workers with respect, give them a sense of worth and appreciation for the task they were recruited to perform, and give them the freedom to innovate. Concentrate on your internal clients; they will handle the rest.

Start with a strong sense of self.

If you are unsure of how folks you are attempting to reach view you, developing a highly successful brand strategy is almost difficult. Understanding your unique company worth is crucial, but it differs from just bragging to people about how amazing you are at what you do. Do not mix up the two. Major businesses spend a lot of money on focus groups for this reason.

Set Yourself Apart From the Competition

Brands that fill an unmet demand in the market stand out from the competition. One that connects with passion and honesty, one that they boldly capture and communicate to the audience. However, a lot of brand managers are reluctant to try new things or go into the uncharted. Being comparable to the opposition is fatal. The market craves novelty, so give it to them and they'll purchase.

How to Create a Tagline and Logo:

7 Tips Focus.

Make it Meaningful:

- Communicate a Message Your Target Audience Will Take care about and Understand.

- Make it Memorable.

- Keep it Short.

- Say It Out Loud.

- Integrate It Into Your Logo Design. Make It Yours.

- What Makes A Logo Design Memorable?

- Important Elements of Creating a Memorable Logo Design You must make sure that your logo design is simple but distinctive.

Create a digital presence for yourself

In 2023, we discovered that nothing is certain when it comes to small enterprises. Businesses have changed, business models have been upended, and consumer habits and behaviors have changed. Adopting new technology and embracing digital methods played a large part in many of these improvements.

Let's now look at how using digital tactics may assist you in creating a strong online presence, connecting with more new clients, strengthening bonds with your current clientele, and raising the profile of your whole business. You must reach consumers where they are now, which is online, since consumer behavior has evolved.

18

Choose the finest website builder for the website of your small company.

You may get your website up using one of the various website builders available. Some rely on a fundamental grasp of design and coding, while others take care of it for you.

Invest in a domain

If you want to create trust online and persuade customers that you are the real deal, your business needs a domain name. Owning your own domain name both enhances your search engine ranking and protects your brand.

Think of your domain name as the internet version of your physical location. It decides how people will find you online.

What should your domain name be, then? When picking a domain name, try to keep it as brief and relevant to your business as you can. To encourage customers to return (and maybe recommend it to their friends!), make sure it is relevant for your business, easy to find, and preferably easy to remember.

There are a number of things to avoid when choosing your domain name, including digits, hyphens, and abbreviations. Of course, it's also very important to make sure you can really purchase the desired domain name! There is nothing worse than having your heart set on a domain name and even going so far as to create social media accounts for it, only to find out that it has already been taken.

The Home Page

Consider your website's homepage as the entrance. Here is your chance to create a solid first impression and highlight the key features of your product or service. Keep in mind that consumers don't have a lot of time, and decisions regarding your website are made in only 0.05 seconds (!!!).

When designing your homepage, it's crucial to consider "who is it for?" This is true for both your website and your whole company. Make sure that it is clear on your homepage whether you cater to a certain group or sector. This may be communicated by words, images, or—better yet—both.

Make it very obvious to your visitors what you want them to do after that. Do you want people to buy from you, give you a call, or join your email list? The final page or action that visitors take on your website shouldn't be your homepage.

Your home page's bio

Every owner of a small company has a tale to tell. What motivated you to begin? What issue are you attempting to address? Why do you value your business? You should convey this tale on your about page.

It might sometimes seem uncomfortable or forced to talk about oneself. However, by telling your small business's narrative, you provide prospective clients or supporters an opportunity to discover more about you than they otherwise could. It explains why they should be interested in what you do and what sets your company apart from the competition.

Share any movies and photographs you may have as well. Despite being a well-known face around the Constant Contact office, Dawn at La Provence isn't a fan of having her picture taken or shared online. Although it's recommended, we chose to include La Provence's famous front door instead of a photo of you and your staff on your about page. Dawn provides background information about the shop's history, her rise to ownership, and location underneath the photograph.

Contact page for you

A contact page is basically just necessary to provide your consumers a way to get in touch with you. It's crucial to be clear about what visitors may anticipate from you when they contact you. When will you respond to them again? What do you anticipate they will submit? What details should they be sure to include in their message?

It's a good idea to give details about your contact details and where and when clients may find you. While the majority of individuals will probably use your contact form, others may want an urgent response and would prefer to phone or come see you. This page's inclusion of your address, contact information, and operating hours will make that procedure easier.

How can businesses use social media for marketing?

On social media, you may engage with your customers and monitor what others are saying about your business. Mobile applications, giveaways, and advertising on social media are further potential uses. Social networking might help your business attract customers, get customer feedback, and build customer loyalty.

How many social media be utilized to market to other companies?

How to create a B2B social media marketing strategy that works best

Sync your goals with those of your business.

Be aware of social opportunities.

Keep a watchful eye on your customers.
Use the correct social media platforms.
Create B2B content with a novel viewpoint in mind.
To determine your progress, analyze your statistics.

What exactly does SEO marketing entail?

Search engine optimization (SEO) is the practice of positioning your website to show up higher on an SERP (search engine results page) in order to attract more visitors. Aiming for rankings for keywords on the first page of search engine results for the market you are targeting is standard practice.
Describe SEO. How does it function?

The art and science of improving a page's position in search engines like Google is called web optimization (SEO). As search is one of the primary ways consumers discover content online, a website's traffic may increase if it ranks better in search engines.

How can SEO be used to market a company?

8 SEO tips for small businesses

1. Pick logical keywords.
2. Be aware of your unique items.
3. Build links to your website instead than cramming it with keywords.
4. Produce a ton of top-notch,
5. Publishable material.
6. Engage in social media activity.
7. Make sure your website is easy to navigate.
8. Analyze the results.

What is a strategy for promoting content?

The practice that passing on blog articles and other resources by means of both paid and unpaid channels. Thus, such as influencer publicity, PR, electronic mail marketing, social media, and syndication, is known as content advertising.

What does marketing with corporate content involve?

A kind of advertising known as "content marketing" involves creating and spreading online content with the intention of motivating readers to visit a brand's website rather than just promoting it. The use of storytelling and information sharing helps increase brand recognition.

How could content marketing be used to promote my business?

1. How to Use Content Marketing to Grow Your Business
2. Determine Your Market's Target.
3. Search for relevant terms.
4. Choose and distribute your resources.

5. You should schedule your material.
6. Create Content.
7. Promote to the Audience You Desire.
8. Add up the results.

What marketing-related approaches do social media aid?

Buffer-based social media marketing

Some businesses embrace social media to promote awareness of their brands, while others use it to boost sales and website traffic. Using social media may also help you create a community, improve your brand's visibility, and provide clients a method to get in touch with you for customer support.

Which five methods of social media platforms marketing are there?

Five Pointers for Effective Social Media Marketing

Make a plan of action. Every platform requires a unique approach.

Be dependable. Although regularity in publishing varies on the platform, it's always a good idea to submit information often.

Create Interesting & Engaging Content to Increase Engagement.

Metrics tracking and analysis.

Which digital marketing is most effective for companies?

- Facebook,
- Twitter,
- Instagram,
- LinkedIn,
- Snapchat,
- And
- Pinterest

Are a few of the most widely used platforms for building brands and conducting marketing campaigns?

What is email marketing for promotion?

Definition. A promotional email is one that is sent to the mailing list that advertises your new or existing products or services. Promotional messages are sent out to let people know about new material, specials, or deals.

How email marketing works?

Email marketing may be used to update subscribers to the list you manage about fresh products, discounts, and other services. Another more subtle marketing strategy is to inform your audience of the advantages of your company or keep their attention after the sale.

Which four sorts of email marketing are there?

Here are 4 excellent email marketing strategies you may use, along with some examples.

Email bulletins. Email newsletters, also known as transactional email, are one of the most widespread and well-liked email marketing initiatives.

Retention emails. Promotional emails.

How may email marketing be used to promote a company?

Advice on designing a profitable email marketing campaign

Select a relevant mailing list.

Create your email.

Personalize the subject line and body of your email.

Be kind and engaging.

Set up follow-ups.

Emails should be sent by a genuine person.

Run an A/B test on your emails.

Observe email rules to avoid spam.

What is sponsored promotion in advertising?

Digital Marketing Lesson: Paid Promotion - DMI

Any media placement or space must be purchased in order for material to be paid for marketing. They're usually advertisements or advertorials that are specific to your audience segmentation. Paid advertising is a fantastic way to determine the effectiveness of your content and the audience response to your marketing message.

What kind of advertisements is paid?

What Advantages Do Paid Ads Offer?

Online advertising that one purchases is known as paid advertising, as the name indicates.

Pay-Per-Click (PPC), programmatic advertising such as Google Ads, Google Display, Facebook Ads, Youtube Ads, LinkedIn Ads, Google and Facebook retargeting, and more are a few examples of paid advertisements.

How can I market my company while earning money?

If nothing else, it will give you inspiration to come up with new, original methods to be paid to promote.

Link up with a car advertising company. Sell ad space on your podcast. Sell ad space on your website.

Sell the lock screen on your phone.

Review products on social media sites.

Become a powerful influence.

Send out guest posts.

How can I get influencers to endorse my company?

Explaining why you believe they would be a good match for your company is the secret to how to attract influencers to endorse your items. Explain to the content producer why you like it and how it supports your campaign's objectives and brand values.

What benefits can influencer marketing provide companies?

Working with influencers may help your company generate internet buzz. Additionally, it may boost audience engagement, your brand's reputation, and conversion rates. It's about time marketers and company owners understood the value of influencer marketing and took use of it.

What do corporate collaborative partnerships entail?

Collaborations are arrangements and acts between organizations that agree to share resources in order to achieve a common objective. Collaborations need the involvement of at least two parties who are willing to exchange resources including money, information, and people.

What role do partnerships and collaborations have in the corporate world?

Collaboration has several advantages, and when done successfully, it may greatly increase employee engagement, wellbeing, and productivity. A collaborative company needs three essential elements in order to succeed: a collaborative culture, the right technologies, and clearly stated goals.

What is brand marketing via business collaboration?

How to Grow Your Instagram Following through Brand Collaborations...

Brand x brand partnerships take place when two or more companies work together to produce something distinctive and original for a campaign and, in the process, support one another's expansion.

Local marketing strategy: what is it?

Local marketing aims to reach people who live in the same city or area as your company. This part of your marketing strategy is targeted towards customers who might potentially buy your goods or services at any time and are located within a certain radius of your actual company location, usually based on an attainable driving distance.

How can I advertise my company in my neighborhood?

- How to advertise locally for your company
- Join regional organizations.
- Run tournaments and competitions.
- Offer local perks and incentives.
- Join forces with nearby influencers and companies.
- Include your company in all local directories.
- Put your logo on the cars.
- Sponsor a group or activity

What are testimonials and reviews?

Reviews are consumers' sincere, impulsively expressed opinions about their purchases, whether favorable or unfavorable. On the other hand, testimonials are just positive client anecdotes that have been gathered with marketing in mind.

What does a promotion testimonial entail?

Examples of Testimonials in Advertising You Should Steal, You Can...

A customer's remark about how a product or service has helped them typically involves their promoting it. This is known as an endorsement testimonial. One of the finest methods to sell your company is via testimonial advertising, which leverages these real client testimonials in the ad language and creativity.

How do you make advantage of consumer feedback and endorsements?

- Place testimonials on landing pages.
- Include testimonials in marketing emails.
- Use client testimonials in your sponsored advertisements.
- Integrate evaluations into your blog.
- Place evaluations close to the CTA.
- Post evaluations on social media.

- Adapt consumer testimonials into success tales.
- Do not discount negative ratings.

What approach does the marketing analysis employ?

A marketing analysis is what? A marketing assessment is a procedure that enables you to comprehend your target market's numerous demographics and audience segmentation, as well as successful engagement tactics, the customer journey, and conversion optimization techniques.

What are the four different sorts of marketing tactics?

Traditional and internet-based advertising, personal selling, direct selling, public relations, sponsorships, and sales promotions are examples of promotional strategy types.

How can I promote my company offline?

Business cards for your small business: offline marketing concepts. One of the best methods to promote your company is to spend money on quality business cards.

Make flyers and brochures.

Create a book, rebrand, distribute discounts, etc.

Send out holiday cards and presents.

Cross-promotion. Participation in the community.

Customer engagement loyalty programs: what are they?

How to Increase Participation in Customer Loyalty Programs...

A systematic customer retention approach that aims to reward customers is a customer loyalty program. It seeks to persuade people to continue purchasing from your company rather than your rivals. Additionally, it promotes client confidence in your brand.

What benefits can customer loyalty programs provide for businesses?

Through unique incentives, loyalty programs may assist businesses in keeping their most important clients. They may also collect vital marketing data, boost referrals, and do other things. Marketers also like loyalty programs, so it's not only customers that do.

What are customer loyalty programs and how are they used by businesses?

A loyalty program is what? Customers that contact with a brand often are rewarded with customer loyalty programs. It's a method for keeping clients by enticing them to keep purchasing from your company rather than one of your rivals. Customers get more incentives the more they spend or interact with the company.

<u>Happy Reading</u>

www.ingramcontent.com/pod-product-compliance
Lightning Source LLC
Chambersburg PA
CBHW071127260726
48661CB00006B/2712